UNSAID FEELINGS

KALYAN KUMAR

Contents

Mr. KALYAN KUMARSILVER MEADLIST NEW YORK MCS AWARD 2022.

The traveller has to knock

at every alien door to come to his own,

and one has to wander through all the outer worlds

to reach the innermost shrine at the end.

-from the poem*journey home* by **Rabindranath Tagore**

Author

ABOUT THE AUTHOR

Mr. Kalyan is an award winning author, poet and song writer from India. Kalyan Kumar is the youngest writer to have a contract from MCS New York. He is also the youngest to be nominated for the best book of the year award. He has been awarded with best seller writer twice within a year. He won the second place in MCS book awards held in New York 2022. Five of his books are 'The Magic Of Words' , 'Meri Manzil' , 'The Journey To Freedom' , 'The Art Of Poetry' and 'Poverty In India'. 'Unsaid Feelings' is his 6th book.

Poem Of Poet

A poet portrayed a picture

Having millions of stories in one

Some related to it

And some drawn a world of another sun

Some had feelings deep

Some had imaginary night with the stolen sleep

Some lines were just chill as water

But some lighted fire

Some that the truth depicted

Some had a fantasy sketched

After all, whatever the poet wrote

Was all a part of the world

Which would ever apart

It was his deep voice peeping outside

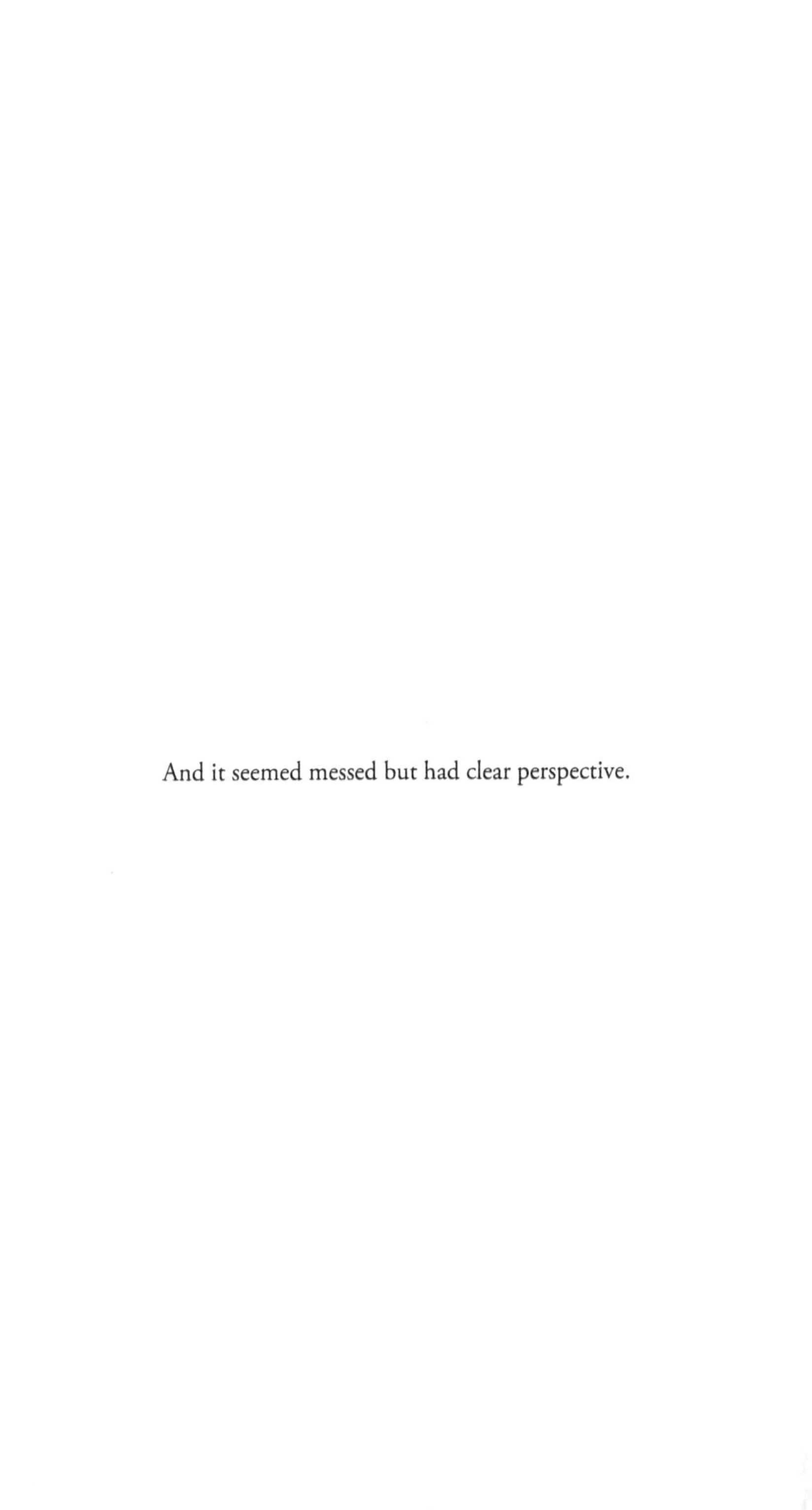

And it seemed messed but had clear perspective.

In His Mind

What reincarnation was

He used to wonder

Travelling past was adventurous

That idea thrilled him.

He was deep into the land of fantasy

Used to imagine what life to be

The supernatural spirit's story

The secret behind night's glory.

The magic amazed him

He believed in miracle

The world beyond universe

Was used to be his imagination!

Express Yourself

I also want to see the world

I also want to see sunrise.

Sometimes also want to answer

Instead of just hidding aside

I also want to reach on the top

And once want to feel the pride.

Want to see my parents priceless smile

While I get any prize.

But I am afraid to show myself

Just feel a little uncomfortable

Unable to express myself

to show the world how much I am capable

But for one thing I feel proud on me

That the only thing I hide is my

tiny little thought.

I am atleast not like those I see

Roses from out and inside bushes of thorns,

The people who are big with money and wealth

But there thoughts are so small.

But I am one of those books

Which is open to all.

Rays Of Freedom

From the dusk to the dawn

From earth to the sky

From poor to the rich

One day the rays of freedom will Conqueror.

Oppressors will get oppressed

By the buds of the dark roses

The sky will again rain happiness

The blood of roses will kill away darkness.

The tears in eyes will dry out

The blood of matyers

The prayers of mothers

Will bear fruits for the oppressed.

The bloody nights, dark stars

Sky is bleeding holding the rain

Blood in seas,watering coffins

Hope one day rays will eross the terrain.

Dear Me

Dear me! You re a temper,

Control it, you will get through.

But, do not over control it,

Because you will lose you.

Dear me! You're smile is lovely,

Keep it up even at all time

When you really cant, because,

You might lose it anytime

Dear me! Never trust your friends!

They are the world, it appears.

But all friendships last no longer

Than a handful of years.

Dear me! Youre strong and powertu.

You're a beast of strengths.

But remember you gain them

Only through life's length's and breath's.

Unknown Girl

A girl walking with ice in her heart

With questions in her mind

With water in her eyes

With pain that no one can see.

She's as pure as the snow on the Himalayas,

And quiet just like the lake.

She's as bright as the moon

With a little yellowish shade.

Is she a ignored girl?

Who is filled with shame?

Or is she a silent girl?

Without any name?

Like a fairy

I wished I had wings

Like a fairy in fairy tale

I wished I would fly high

Like a fairy in fairy tale.

I would have embrace

The world with love

I would been selfiess

And helping others.

Would have no fear

And could use super powers

Just like a fairy tale

World would have been magical.

My Dreams

My Dreams aren't big,

But not even small

I live an independent life,

And say that's all!

I go to my dream working space,

With a bag in my hand,

And,My head held high!

I wanna live my dream,

And just wanna fly!

I see countless inspiring men,

Doing best in their field,

But also the talented men,

Who just only dreamed!

Both are my motivation

In numnerous ways,

I look up to them,

In my tough days.

I want to travel the world,

And reach to the sky.

I want to live in my own home,

And do not want to rely.

Maybe it's hard,

But I really want to try.

I wanna live my dreamn,

And just wanna fly!

My Life

World is made of love,

And there is nothing above.

Nature is full of beauty,

And it's our prime duty.

Everyone left me,

But my heart assisted me.

I loved everyone from outside,

But everything was dull inside.

No one loved me,

But I was with me.

No one trusted me,

But I was with me.

So, today I am having fun

With no more feelings for anyone.

Cloudy Sunshine

It's cloudy outside,

It's cloudy in my brain.

Doubts are stacking up,

They are driving me insane.

It's raining outside,

It's raining inside me.

Water rising up quickly,

Conveys all the memory.

Wind started blowing outside,

Blowing my sorrows away.

Clouds are slowly parting,

I know I am gonna be okay.

Sun Shinning Outside,

I am shining like the sun.

No more sorrows,

My worries are on to run.

Fake Friends

What all it takes

To be a snake

Just know the person

And be a poison.

Life is tough

These snakes make it rough

The one you have faith in

Will not let you win.

A small reminder to them

Karma is always set

Thanks for being Yourself

Now wait and regret.

Me And The Moon

The witching hour

Will be here soon

No one's around

It's just me and the moon.

Luminosity shining bright

A glowing gif,A beautiful sight

An ancient lantern

In the sky

My one true love

Way up high.

Don't need a day break

Morning or noon

Happily alone

Just me and the moon.

Middle Aged Dreamer

A man without purpose

And no particular theme

Just a middle aqed dreamer

With a middle aged dream.

No plans of action

A defeatist with no scheme

Just a middle aged dreamer

With a midde aged dream.

Never part of the group

Or any Cliquish team

Just a midde aged dreamer

With a middle aged dream.

Maybe a loving touch

Nothing tO extreme

JUst a middle aged dreamer

With a middle aged dream.

Wishing that the darkrness would lift

And could enjoy the sunny beams

Just a middle aged dreamer

With silly middle aged dreams.

Self Worth

Make your self worth dear

If you don't no one will be here

You have to work continuosly

To build up your image flawlessly

You have the opportunity

Please be a little witty

Once you will be there

Everyone else will take care.

Life is not small

And you are not a pictured doll

Mate, you have to crawl

And even fall, all this to stand tall

Pebbles are nothing on your way

You need to handle all that to slay

Make your self worth now

And see everyone bow.

Nightmare

Should I curse you

Or shall thank you

For offering haunted day

And making me stronger today.

Should I remember the secret you told me

My untold story that is unknown to me

Or should I ignore what you said in my sleep

And live in the illusion I made.

Should I believe in you

And make you my saviour

Or keep you as my weakness

And cherish fear of you forever.